🐾 Why is grass green?

When light hits something, only some of its colors bounce back. Grass looks green because only green light bounces off it— the other colors of light are swallowed up.

Why is the sky blue?

PaRRagon

Bath · New York · Singapore · Hong Kong · Cologne · Delhi
Melbourne · Amsterdam · Johannesburg · Auckland · Shenzhen

Acknowledgements
Cover images from iStockphoto, all internal images from iStockphoto

First published by Parragon in 2011

Parragon
Queen Street House
4 Queen Street
Bath BA1 1HE, UK

ISBN 978-1-4454-5949-3

Printed in China

CONTENTS

OUR PLANET

☼ What's special about our planet?

As far as we know, Earth is the only planet in the solar system that has life. As well as warmth from the sun, the other main ingredient for life is liquid water. Earth has plenty of water—in total, it covers about three-fourths of the planet's surface!

Precious water

Planet earth

☼ What does Earth look like from space?

It looks beautiful—blue with swirling white clouds. Astronauts in space spend most of their free time gazing at it. They can even make out cities, when they are lit up at night with twinkling lights.

DISCOVERY FACT™

When Earth first formed, it was extremely hot and there was no oxygen. Over millions of years, the planet cooled, oceans formed, and oxygen was made. The first life on Earth appeared more than 3 billion years ago.

 Why does our sky get dark at night?

Like all planets, the Earth is spinning as it orbits the Sun. When your part of the planet is facing away from the Sun, its light is blocked out. At the same time, it is daytime for people on the opposite side of the Earth.

AIR

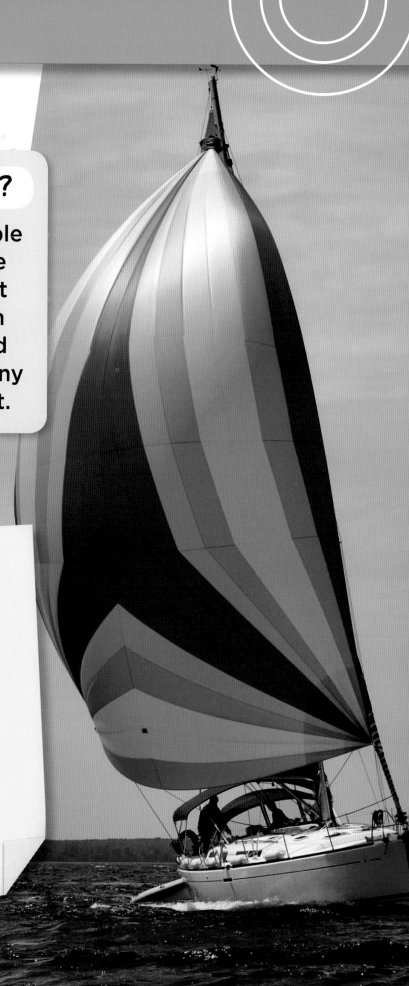

What is air made of?

Air is a mixture of invisible gases. The main ones are nitrogen and oxygen, but there's also some carbon dioxide, water vapor, and other gases, as well as tiny bits of salt, dust, and dirt.

☼ **How do we Know air is there?**

We can't see or taste or smell air, but we can feel and hear it when the wind blows. Wind is moving air—it's what makes trees bend and leaves rustle, and what blows sailboats across the water.

Balloon full of air

☼ Is there air in space?

The skin of air around the Earth is called the atmosphere, and it fades away into nothingness high above the ground. 'Space' begins around 100km (62 miles) above us. There's no air in space, but most of the other planets have their own atmospheres, which are quite different to ours.

Floating astronaut

OUR SUN

How hot is the Sun?

In deserts here on Earth, heat that has traveled 93 million miles (150 million km) from the Sun can be hot enough to fry an egg. The Sun's surface is a super-hot 10,830°F (6,000°C), and its center or core is even hotter.

Hot desert

Spots on the Sun

Is the Sun all one color?

The Sun is not the same color all over. Some areas of its surface are darker. These spots are little pockets that are slightly cooler.

The Sun is a star—a gigantic ball of burning gas. It has been shining for about five billion years.

Total eclipse

☀ When does the Sun go out?

When there's a total eclipse. This happens when the Moon's path takes it between the Earth and the Sun, and the Moon casts a shadow across the surface of the Earth.

STARRY SKY

How are stars born?

The gases in a nebula (cloud of dust and gas) gradually gather together into spinning balls. They spin more and more quickly, until they get amazingly hot, and a big blast, called a nuclear reaction, begins. When this happens, a baby star begins to glow.

What are stars made of?

Stars are mostly made of two gases, hydrogen and helium. Helium is the gas used to fill party balloons. There are lots of layers inside a star, with gases moving around in each one.

Helium balloons

Close-up of star

How long do stars shine for?

Very hot, bright stars burn up all their energy in a few million years. A star like our Sun, which is only medium-hot, can shine for billions of years.

Everything in space, including you, is made out of elements, such as carbon and silicon. All of these elements were cooked up in the stars, so we are made of stardust!

OUR MOON

☀ Why does the Moon change shape?

It doesn't really—it's ball-shaped just like Earth. As the Moon travels around Earth, you see different amounts of its sunlit half. It seems to change gradually from a crescent to a disk, and back again.

Craters

☀ Why does the Moon have so many craters?

Because it has been pelted by so many space rocks and has no atmosphere to protect it. One of the biggest craters, named Bailly, is nearly 186 miles (300 km) across. You can make out some of the craters on the Moon using a good pair of binoculars.

Jumping on the Moon

What is the dark side of the Moon?

It's the part of the Moon that we can never see from Earth. The Moon takes the same time to orbit the Earth as it does to spin once. This means the same side of the Moon always faces away from the Earth.

Crescent Moon

COLORS OF NATURE

☼ Is light white?

Light may look white sometimes, but it's really a mixture of all the colors of the rainbow—red, orange, yellow, green, blue, indigo (violet-blue), and violet.

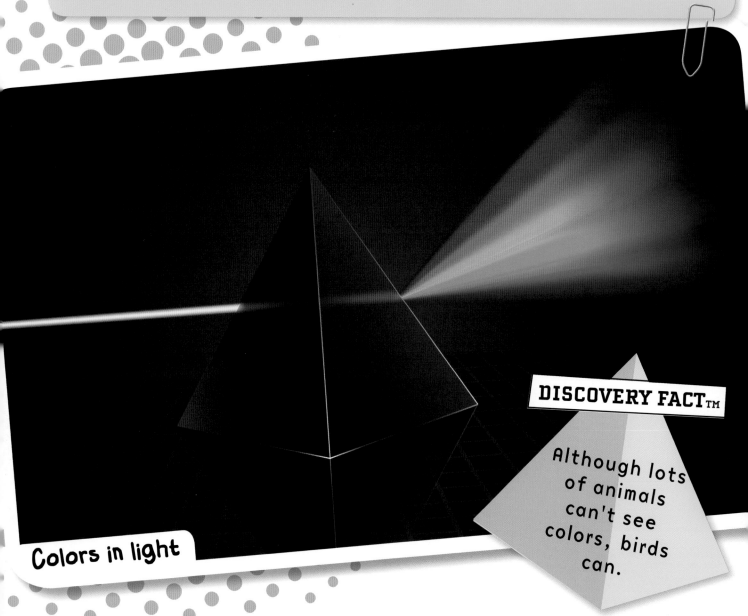

Colors in light

DISCOVERY FACT™

Although lots of animals can't see colors, birds can.

☀ Why do rainbows happen?

Rainbows happen when sunlight passes through water drops. The water drops make white light spread into all its colors, and we see a rainbow.

☀ Why is the sky blue?

Blue light has a short wavelength so most of it is absorbed by gas molecules and scattered in different directions. Whichever direction you look, some of this scattered blue light reaches you, making the sky look blue.

MOUNTAINS

 How are mountains built?

Some mountains are built when two pieces of the Earth's crust bump or crash into each other. The rock in between is pushed up into giant fold mountains. Other mountains are made when huge blocks of rocks are squeezed up.

Snowcaps

DISCOVERY FACT™

The higher up you go, the colder it gets. That's why the tops of some mountain peaks are capped in snow and why many mountain animals have warm winter coats.

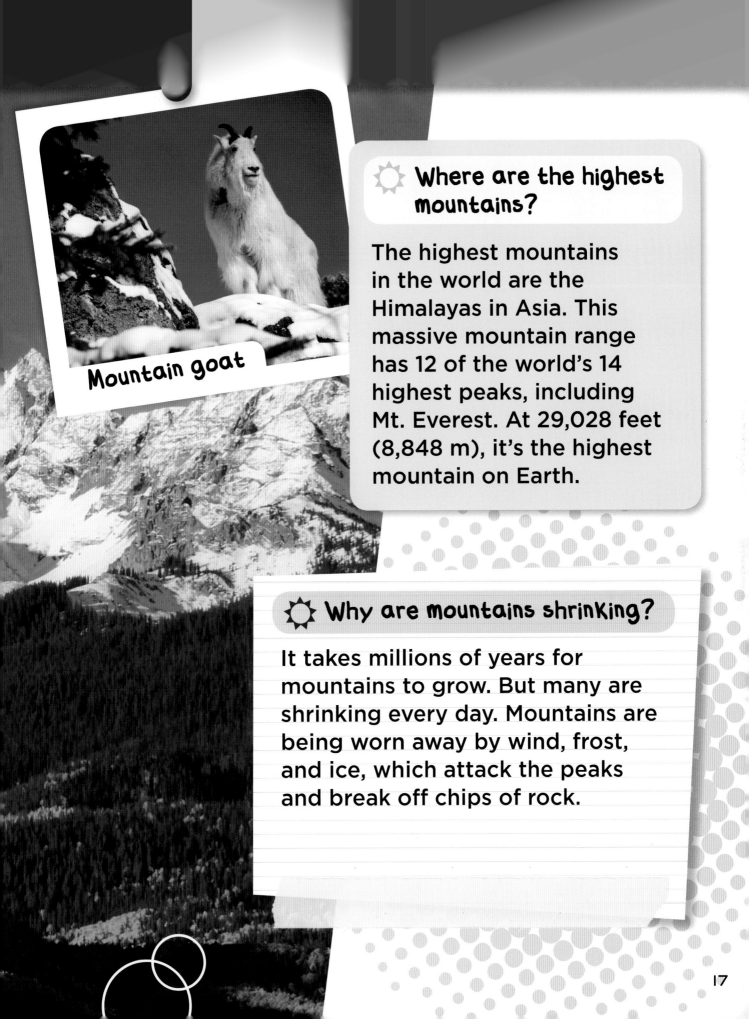

Mountain goat

☼ Where are the highest mountains?

The highest mountains in the world are the Himalayas in Asia. This massive mountain range has 12 of the world's 14 highest peaks, including Mt. Everest. At 29,028 feet (8,848 m), it's the highest mountain on Earth.

☼ Why are mountains shrinking?

It takes millions of years for mountains to grow. But many are shrinking every day. Mountains are being worn away by wind, frost, and ice, which attack the peaks and break off chips of rock.

THE POLES

☼ Where are the Poles?

The North and South Poles are at either end of the Earth. The North Pole is surrounded by the frozen Arctic Ocean. The South Pole is in the middle of icy Antarctica.

North Pole

South Pole

☼ Why are the Poles cold?

The poles are the coldest places on Earth. They're battered by blizzards and covered in ice and snow. The poles are cold because the Sun's rays hit them at a slant, so they're spread out and very weak.

☼ Do penguins live at the North Pole?

No, penguins only live around the South Pole. But you might bump into a polar bear at the North Pole.

DISCOVERY FACT™

The coldest place on Earth is Vostok in Antarctica. Here temperatures can plummet to a freezing -128°F (-89°C).

Penguin

Polar bear

THE SEA

☼ How big is the sea?

The sea is absolutely huge! Salty sea water covers about two-thirds of our planet so there's far more sea than land. The sea lies in five oceans—the Pacific, Atlantic, Indian, Arctic and Southern Oceans.

Diver Under the Sea

☼ Which is the biggest ocean?

By far the biggest ocean is the vast Pacific. It alone covers a third of the Earth. At its widest point, between Panama and Malaysia, it stretches almost halfway around the world.

DISCOVERY FACT™

The first person to set sail around the world was Ferdinand Magellan. He set off from Spain in 1519.

☀ Why is the sea salty?

The sea's salty taste comes from ordinary salt. It's the same stuff you sprinkle on your food. The rain washes the salt out of rocks on land and the rivers carry it into the sea. People then collect the salt left after the water dries.

Pacific ocean

Sea salt

THE SEA

☀ Why does the sea flow in and out?

Twice a day, the sea washes onto the shore at high tide. Then it flows back out again at low tide. The tides are caused by the Moon and Sun pulling the sea into giant bulges on either side of the Earth.

Low tide

Sandy beach

☀ Why are beaches sandy?

Sand is made from tiny fragments of rock and shells, crushed up by the wind and water. Sand is usually yellow or white. But some sand is black because it contains volcanic rock or coal.

DISCOVERY FACT™

If all the coasts were straightened out, they'd stretch round the Earth 13 times. At 56,000 miles (90,000 km), Canada has the longest coast.

☀ How are cliffs carved out?

Along the coast, the rocks are worn away by the force of the waves. As the waves crash against the shore, they carve out cliffs, caves, and high arches. Sometimes an arch collapses, leaving a stack or pillar of rock.

DESERTS

 Why are deserts dry?

Deserts are the driest places on Earth. In some deserts, it doesn't rain for years at a time. In others, it never rains at all. Some deserts are also scorching hot. In the daytime, the sand's hot enough to fry an egg on.

Camel in the Sahara

Can sand dunes move?

Strong winds blowing across the desert pile the sand up into giant heaps, or dunes. The biggest stand 650 feet (200 m) tall. The dunes creep forward every year and can bury whole desert villages.

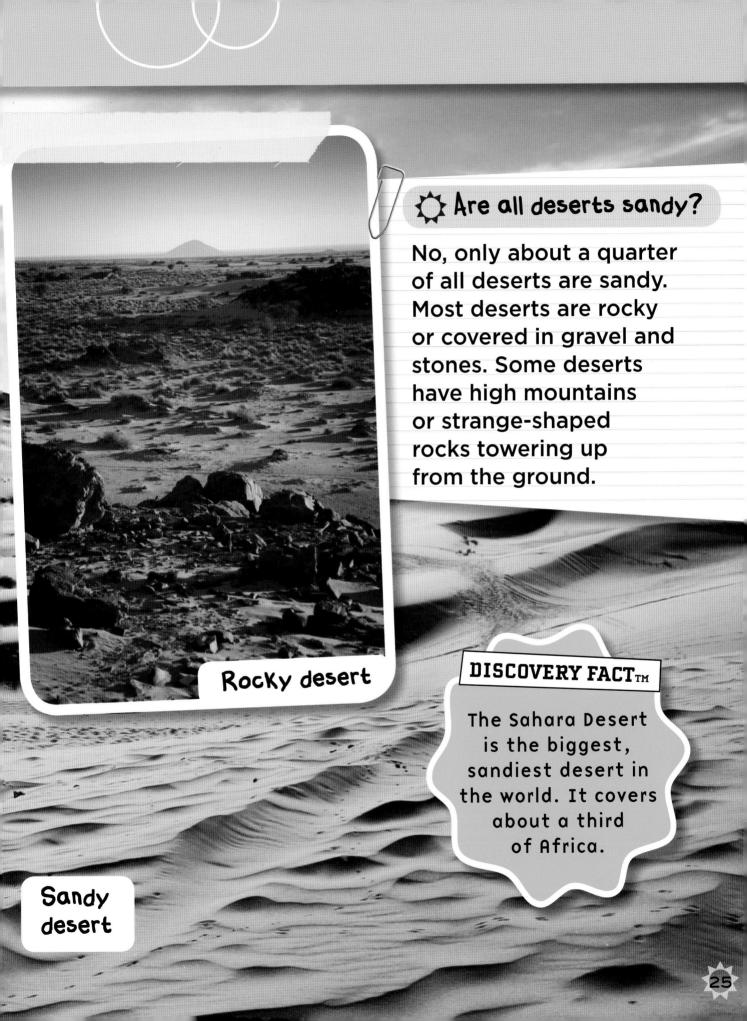

☼ Are all deserts sandy?

No, only about a quarter of all deserts are sandy. Most deserts are rocky or covered in gravel and stones. Some deserts have high mountains or strange-shaped rocks towering up from the ground.

Rocky desert

DISCOVERY FACT™

The Sahara Desert is the biggest, sandiest desert in the world. It covers about a third of Africa.

Sandy desert

PLANTS

Sunflowers

☼ What is a plant?

A plant is a living thing, just like you. Like all living things, plants grow, breathe, feed, and make babies. Unlike animals, plants can use their leaves, roots, stems, and flowers to make the food they need to grow. Mushrooms and other fungi aren't plants because they don't need sunlight to grow.

Mushrooms

☼ Why do plants have roots?

A plant needs roots to hold it in the soil so that it doesn't blow over in the wind. Tall trees need longer, stronger roots than small flowering plants. Roots also suck up water from the soil and carry it up the trunk or stem to the rest of the plant.

Roots

Sunlight

☼ What do plants need to grow?

Plants need sunlight, water, air, and space to grow. Most plants will die if they are left in the dark or uprooted from damp soil.

DISCOVERY FACT™

Some plants grow on other plants, not in the soil. These plants are called epiphytes. They include beautiful orchid flowers.

LEAVES

Types of leaves

☼ Why do plants have leaves?

Because leaves work hard, making food for the plant to grow. Green leaves contain a green coloring called chlorophyll. The chlorophyll uses sunlight and a gas from the air, called carbon dioxide, to change water into a kind of sugar. The sugar feeds the plant. This way of making food is called photosynthesis.

☀ Why do some leaves change color in the fall?

Green leaves change color when their green coloring, or chlorophyll, breaks down. Other colors then show through and the leaves look brown, red, or yellowy gold.

☀ Why do plants have stems?

Stems grow toward the sunlight and support the plants' leaves, so that they can make food. Stems also carry water, minerals, and sugary food (called sap) around the plant. Some plants have straight stems, others are curly.

DISCOVERY FACT™

Plants "sweat." During photosynthesis, plants give off water. Just look at the water on the windows of a greenhouse!

TREES

Fallen leaves

☀ Why do trees lose their leaves?

Some trees lose their leaves in the wintertime when there is less sunlight and water freezes in the ground. These trees, called deciduous trees, rest during the winter. They store enough food during the summer to keep themselves alive until the following spring when new leaves grow.

What are growing rings?

A growing ring is added to a tree's trunk every year. The ring is thick if the tree has grown a lot during a warm, long summer with plenty of rain, and thin if the tree has not grown much because the weather has been harsh.

Growing rings

DISCOVERY FACT™

Plants sleep. Green plants can only make food during the day when there's lots of sunlight. At night, they shut down and rest.

Do all trees lose their leaves?

No—some trees keep their leaves all year round. They are called evergreens because they are always, or forever, green. They include spruces and pine trees.

Pine trees

Why are rain forests so wet?

Because it rains almost every single day! In the late afternoon, the sky turns black and there's a heavy thunderstorm. Rain forests grow along the equator where it's hot and sticky all year round. It's perfect weather for plants to grow.

Where do the biggest forests grow?

The biggest forests in the world stretch for thousands of miles across the north of Europe and Asia. The trees that grow here are conifers. They're trees with needlelike leaves and cones.

Deep in the rain forest

How do rain forests grow?

Rain forests grow in layers depending on the height of the trees. The tallest trees poke out above the forest. Below them is a thick roof of treetops called the canopy. Next comes a layer of shorter trees, herbs, and shrubs.

Layers of trees

DISCOVERY FACT™

The biggest rain forest grows in South America along the banks of the Amazon River. It's home to millions of plants and animals.

Tree Frog

FLOWERS

☀ **Why do plants have flowers?**

Most plants have colorful flowers to attract birds, bats, and lots of different kinds of insects, such as beetles, butterflies, and bees. These animals help the plants make seeds to grow new plants.

Field of flowers

Why do flowers smell?

Sweet-smelling flowers help to attract animals. The scent tells insects and other animals that the flower contains a sweet, sugary juice called nectar, which the animals like to drink.

Bee on flower

Rafflesia plant

DISCOVERY FACT™

The rafflesia plant smells like rotten meat! This attracts flies that like pungent smells.

How are seeds made?

Flowers have male parts called stamens and female parts called carpels. The stamens make tiny grains of pollen. The carpels contain eggs, called ovules. Seeds are made when the pollen reaches the ovules. This is called pollination.

DEADLY PLANTS

☀ Are some plants dangerous?

Some plants are poisonous to stop animals eating them. Poisonous plants include foxgloves, lupins, and deadly nightshade. Poison ivy may leave blisters if it touches bare skin. Nettles have tiny hairs on their leaves that inject you with poison if you brush against them.

Deadly nightshade

Rose with thorns

☀ Which plants have weapons?

Brambles and roses have thorns, cacti have sharp spines, and holly has spiky leaves, to stop animals from eating them.

Venus Flytrap

☀ Which plants eat meat?

Some plants eat insects as well as making their own food. When an insect touches a delicate hair on the inside of the leaves of a Venus flytrap, the leaves snap shut, trapping the insect inside. Insects landing on the edge of the pitcher plant slip into a pool of liquid at the bottom and drown.

DISCOVERY FACT™

Potatoes

USEFUL PLANTS

☼ Which plants can we eat?

We can eat all kinds of plants. We eat the leaves, roots, and stalks of vegetable plants and all kinds of fruits and nuts. Sugar, spices, breakfast cereals, and even chocolate come from plants.

Cereals

Cotton plant

☀ How do plants help us?

Plants give us lots of other things as well as food. Cotton cloth comes from the cotton plant and linen comes from a plant called flax. Plants are also used to make oil, beauty products, and medicines.

Cotton clothes

VOLCANOES

Volcano erupti

☼ Why do volcanoes blow their tops?

Volcanoes are mountains that spit fire. Deep under the Earth, there is red-hot, runny rock called magma. Sometimes the magma bursts up through a crack in the Earth's crust and a volcano erupts.

Flowing lava

☀ What is lava?

Once magma has erupted from a volcano, it is called lava. Some lava is thick and lumpy. Some is thin and runny. In the air, it cools and turns into hard, black rock.

☀ Does volcanic ash move?

Clouds of gas and ash can flow across the ground at more than 100mph (160 kph)—that's as fast as a train!

DISCOVERY FACT™

Some of the world's highest mountains are volcanoes. They include Mt. Kilimanjaro in Africa, which is now extinct.

Mt. Kilimanjaro

EARTHQUAKES

☼ What makes the Earth shake?

The Earth's surface is cracked into enormous pieces that drift on the red-hot, runny rock below. Sometimes two pieces push and shove each other, making the Earth shake.

☼ How much damage do earthquakes cause?

Big earthquakes do lots of damage. Huge cracks open up in the ground. Houses, roads, and bridges shake and fall down. In the worst earthquakes, many people are killed and injured by buildings that collapse on top of them.

Earthquake damage

How do scientists measure an earthquake?

An earthquake sends shock waves rippling through the ground. Scientists study these waves using a Seismograph device to see how big the earthquake is. They measure earthquakes on a scale of 1 to 10.

A Seismograph device

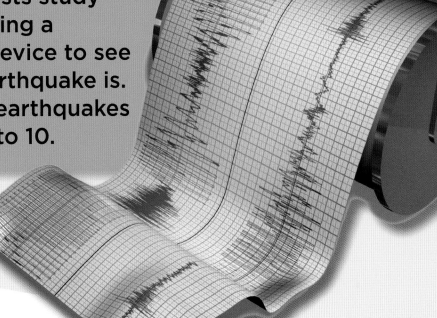

DISCOVERY FACT™

The largest recorded earthquake in the United States was a magnitude 9.2 that struck Prince William Sound, Alaska on March 28, 1964.

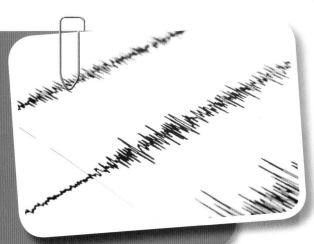

FLOODS

How do Floods happen?

Many floods happen when it rains very heavily and rivers overflow. They burst their banks and flood the land all around. You also get floods in stormy weather when high tides or gigantic waves sweep on the shore.

Flooded town

☼ What are Flash Floods?

Flash floods are floods that happen very suddenly, with no warning. Sometimes there isn't time to evacuate buildings in the flood's path. Flash floods can happen in the desert, too, during a rare downpour of rain.

☀ Are some floods useful?

Yes, the Nile River in Egypt used to flood every year, leaving rich mud on the fields. The mud made the soil ideal for farmers to grow bumper crops. The Nile doesn't flood anymore because a large dam was built to store its water.

Nile river

Flash Flood

DISCOVERY FACT™

In 1955, a flood in New England washed a four-story wooden hotel clean away. Imagine how surprised the guests were when they looked out of their windows!

STORMS

Lightning

☀ When do thunderstorms happen?

Thunderstorms usually happen on a hot summer's day when the air is warm and sticky. Watch out for huge, dark, tall thunderclouds gathering in the sky. They're a sure sign a storm is brewing.

☼ What makes thunder rumble?

Lightning is incredibly hot, about five times hotter than the Sun's surface. As it streaks through the sky, it heats the air so quickly that it makes a loud booming sound. This is the sound of thunder.

Stormy Clouds

DISCOVERY FACT™

Lightning and thunder happen at exactly the same time. But you see lightning before you hear thunder because light travels more quickly than sound.

☼ What makes lightning flash?

Inside a thundercloud, strong winds hurl droplets of water around. They bump and bash into each other. This makes the cloud crackle with static electricity, which builds up and suddenly streaks through the sky as lightning.

INDEX